W9-AZI-977

Looking at . . . Triceratops
A Dinosaur from the CRETACEOUS Period

Weekly Reader®
BOOKS

Published by arrangement with Gareth Stevens, Inc.
Newfield Publications is a federally registered trademark
of Newfield Publications, Inc. Weekly Reader is a federally
registered trademark of Weekly Reader Corporation.

Library of Congress Cataloging-in-Publication Data

Vaughan, Jenny.
    Looking at-- Triceratops/written by Jenny Vaughan; illustrated by Tony Gibbons.
        p.   cm. -- (The New dinosaur collection)
    Includes index.
    ISBN 0-8368-1048-1
    1. Triceratops--Juvenile literature. [1. Triceratops. 2. Dinosaurs.] I. Gibbons, Tony, ill.
II. Title. III. Series.
QE862.O65V38 1993
567.9'7--dc20   93-26033

This North American edition first published in 1993 by
Gareth Stevens Publishing
1555 North RiverCenter Drive, Suite 201
Milwaukee, Wisconsin 53212 USA

This U.S. edition © 1993 by Gareth Stevens, Inc. Created with original © 1993 by
Quartz Editorial Services, Premier House, 112 Station Road, Edgware HA8 7AQ U.K.

Consultant: Dr. David Norman, Director of the Sedgwick Museum of Geology,
University of Cambridge, England.

Printed in the United States of America

Weekly Reader Books Presents

Looking at . . . Triceratops
A Dinosaur from the CRETACEOUS Period

by Jenny Vaughan

Illustrated by Tony Gibbons

THE NEW **DINOSAUR** COLLECTION

Gareth Stevens Publishing
MILWAUKEE

Contents

Introducing Triceratops

Picture a hillside in North America over 65 million years ago. There is a herd of huge, horned creatures wandering across it. These animals are not small creatures like deer or even lumbering buffalo. They are far bigger than any wildlife we know today.

They are **Triceratops** (TRY-SER-A-TOPS), some of the last of the dinosaurs. They died out 65 million years ago, at the same time as all the other dinosaurs that were left on Earth.

Paleontologists (scientists who study the remains of plants and animals that lived millions of years ago) have found the bones of whole herds of **Triceratops**. A live herd of these huge animals must have been a frightening sight.

But why did **Triceratops** need to frighten other creatures? Read on to find the answer to this and many other questions about this extraordinary dinosaur.

Large numbers of bones have been found in Montana in the United States and in Alberta, Canada.

Three-horned dinosaur

Triceratops was a giant, scaly animal. It was as long as two ordinary-sized cars, more than twice your height, and weighed as much as 90 people. It is extinct now; but if the children in the picture could have met **Triceratops**, they would probably have been terrified by this dinosaur.

Perhaps the strangest thing about **Triceratops** was its head, which took up one third of its body length.

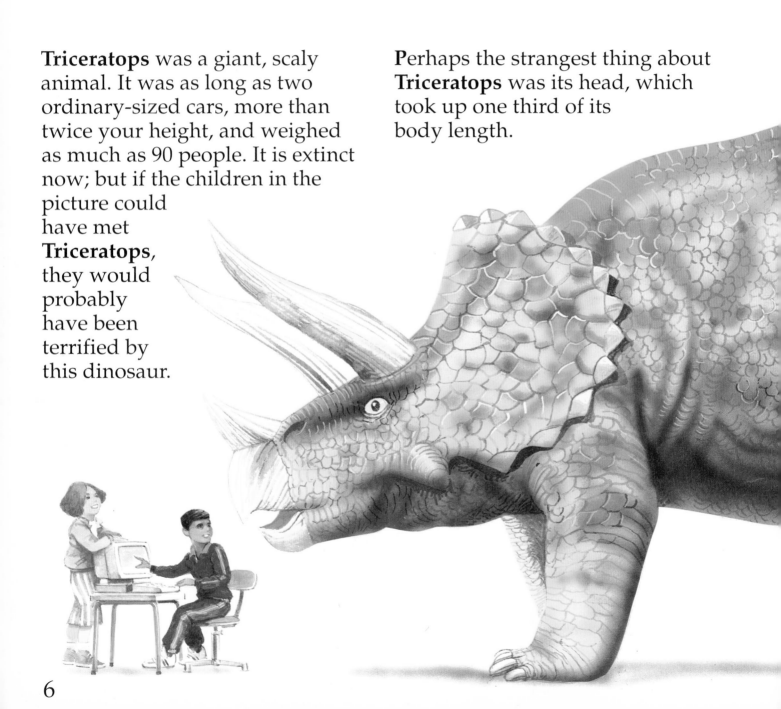

6

Triceratops had three huge horns – one above each of its eyes and one on its nose.

It is because of these horns that this dinosaur was called *Triceratops*, which means "three-horned face." (*Tri* at the beginning of a word always means "three.")

All around its head, Triceratops had a stiff frill of bone covered with skin. Scientists think this may have helped Triceratops defend itself from attack. It may also have been used to show off when attracting mates.

We can tell from its teeth that Triceratops was a plant-eater. It had hundreds of sharp, slicing teeth along the sides of its mouth. As these teeth wore out, new ones grew in their place. At the front of its face, Triceratops had a large, curved beak.

As you can see, Triceratops's head was much bigger than your whole body. It certainly looked fierce but would probably only have attacked in self-defense.

Mighty skeleton

The only way scientists can tell what **Triceratops** looked like is from its bones. The bones show that it looked a little like a rhinoceros. But scientists can also tell, from studying the bones, that **Triceratops** was about five times heavier than a rhinoceros.

The skull shows that its head was large even for its bulky body. **Triceratops** needed strong, sturdy legs to carry its body. Its front legs were shorter than its hind legs, so its back was curved upward toward the hips.

Triceratops walked around on all fours, but not on the flat part of its feet. Instead, it walked on its toes, like a cat or dog.

Its legs were not as long as those of many other dinosaurs, but Triceratops could still probably run very fast. It must have been very frightening for any other dinosaur to be charged by one.

The big horns on the top of Triceratops's head were almost as tall as you are. When Triceratops was alive, the horns were covered with a coating that made them even longer. The nose horn was shorter than the other two.

From marks on the bone of Triceratops's neck frill, scientists know that it was once covered with muscles that stretched to the jaws. This means that one of the frill's jobs may have been to help move Triceratops's jaws as it ate.

The frill also protected its neck and was useful as a sort of shield when Triceratops needed to defend itself against a rival or enemy.

Its tail, as you can see, was long and tapered toward the end. Unlike dinosaurs that walked on two legs, Triceratops did not use its tail for balance.

In Triceratops's time

Triceratops lived toward the end of the Cretaceous Period, which lasted from 135–65 million years ago. In those days, the climate was much warmer than it is now.

In **Triceratops's** time, there were open hillsides with palms and plants called cycads. Groups of **Triceratops** roamed the land. Sometimes, they crossed broad rivers as they went from one feeding ground to another.

Many different dinosaurs roamed the plains with **Triceratops**. All watched out for the approach of predators, such as **Tyrannosaurus rex** (TIE-RAN-OH-SAW-RUS RECKS).

Euoplocephalus (YOO-PLO-SEFF-A-LUS) was well protected from predators. It had a thick, armored skin covered with spikes and a bony tail-club.

If attacked, **Euoplocephalus** would swing its tail at its enemy. A blow with its tail-club would have wounded even the fiercest predator.

But **Ornithomimus** (OR-<u>NITH</u>-OH-<u>MIME</u>-US), a Cretaceous dinosaur that looked like an ostrich, had to rely on its swift legs to get it out of danger.

The sky, meanwhile, was home to flying reptiles – the pterosaurs – and some of the earliest birds.

Triceratops attack!

Triceratops did not have to run from danger. It could easily fight off an attacker, probably in the same way that a rhinoceros does today – by putting its head down and charging its enemy.

Its horns could pierce the tough hide of an attacker, and its muscles were very strong.

With its powerful horns and heavy body, it was a match for the fiercest meat-eaters.

Triceratops could even knock a large carnivore right off its feet.

Triceratops could probably travel at about 25 miles (40 km) per hour – almost as fast as a car is allowed to go in town today.

Once it was running, it would have been very difficult for **Triceratops** to stop quickly.

Few predators would have stayed around to fight with **Triceratops.** It was well protected against predators. Its neck frill shielded its shoulders and back from sharp teeth and claws. Its thick, knobby skin protected it from bites and scratches. A **Triceratops** attack was fast and furious.

Head-wrestlers

Triceratops's horns were sharp and dangerous. They were useful as weapons for driving off predators. But they probably had other uses as well. We can guess what some of these uses may have been by looking at how some of today's creatures behave when using body weapons of this kind.

Deer, for example, have antlers on their heads. The males use these to fight each other by clashing them together in a kind of wrestling match.

The male deer that wins the most matches drives the other males away. He is now left to be leader of the herd – until he is challenged again for the leadership.

We know that **Triceratops** lived in herds because so many bones have been found together in one place.

Millions of years ago, **Triceratops** males may also have fought to see who would be leader of the herd, and also for mates, just like the deer of today.

The neck frills protected **Triceratops** from being slashed by enemies or by the horns of other **Triceratops.**

Scientists have even found marks on **Triceratops** neck frills that show where they became damaged during fights. The sight of two enormous male **Triceratops** crashing into each other and doing battle must have been amazing.

What color was Triceratops?

Many samples of fossilized dinosaur skin have been found. Scientists know that **Triceratops**, at the top of the next page, had very knobby skin. But they have had to make guesses about its color.

Many pictures of dinosaurs show them as brown, gray, or green, like the **Supersaurus** (SUPER-<u>SAW</u>- RUS) on this page. These colors would have blended in with forests or open country, making the dinosaur hard to spot.

Some dinosaurs, like the **Deinonychus** (<u>DIE</u>-NO-<u>NY</u>-KUS) at the bottom of the next page, were fast runners.

There are also blue and red lizards and snakes with bands of brilliant colors. So, there is no reason why some dinosaurs could not have been brightly colored, too.

Some of today's lizards also have big neck frills that the males display to females. These are often highly colored, especially in the mating season. **Triceratops's** frill helped protect it from enemies during attack, but it may also have been used to attract mates.

If **Triceratops** did use the frill in this way, a male's frill may have been much brighter in color than the female's, or even a different color altogether. We may never know for sure.

They could escape easily from predators.

So, it was probably not so important that they blend in with the surroundings. They could have been any color and would still have been safe as long as they were quick on their feet. Scientists think they may even have been striped or spotted.

Many reptiles and birds living today are brightly colored. There are birds with red and pink feathers and even blue feet.

Danger!

A small herd of **Triceratops** was grazing peacefully on a hillside. These dinosaurs spent most of their time searching for food, like all large plant-eaters. They were wandering around, snipping off the leaves and shoots of palm plants with their sharp, hornlike beaks.

What none of them knew, however, was that a huge and hungry **Tyrannosaurus rex** was lurking nearby. It soon saw its chance.

A young **Triceratops** had wandered away from the herd.

Suddenly, **Tyrannosaurus rex** leaped out from its hiding place, its huge mouth open, ready to bite into the body of its victim.

The young **Triceratops** squealed in terror and tried to run away as fast as it could. The adults heard its frightened cry and quickly rushed to the rescue.

With only seconds to spare, the young **Triceratops** dived in among the adults. Members of the herd grouped together, using their bodies to make a wall around the baby. They faced outward, their horns lowered, ready to charge.

Tyrannosaurus rex now knew it had no chance of catching the baby and would probably be killed if it tried. Disappointed, it loped away to look for an easier way of finding a meal.

Triceratops data

A scientist once mistook some **Triceratops** remains for the bones of a giant buffalo – probably because the two horns on the top of **Triceratops's** head were in the same position as buffalo horns.

Scientists think there may have been two or three different kinds of **Triceratops** since some skeletons seem to have had different kinds of horns.

All three horns were dangerous weapons, but they may also have been useful for showing off to mates or to frighten enemies away.

Parrotlike beaks

All **Triceratops** had a beak at the front of their faces. It was curved like a parrot's, but much bigger, and made of hard, hornlike material. **Triceratops** used its beak for cutting through plants.

Knobby skin

Dinosaurs had scaly skin. But the scales did not overlap, like fish scales do. They were more like thick patches of skin.

Triceratops had especially thick skin, even for a dinosaur. The patches formed a pattern and looked a bit like a mosaic of tiles. **Triceratops** also had hornlike points on its cheeks and thick knobs all over its body.

Thick tail

Triceratops's tail was not very long for a dinosaur, but it was thick and muscular, strengthened by stringy rods called tendons.

Several hooves

Instead of having just one hoof on each foot, as some animals do today, **Triceratops** had several. It had three hooves on each front foot, plus two other toes. Each back foot had four toes, with a hoof on each. These hooves protected **Triceratops's** feet from rough ground. There was also a pad behind each back foot, just like rhinoceroses have today. These pads help a rhinoceros walk and run more comfortably, which is probably why **Triceratops** had them, too.

The Ceratopsian family

Triceratops belonged to a family of dinosaurs called the **Ceratopsians.** They lived toward the end of the age of the dinosaurs, in the region we now call North America.

It lived between 70 and 65 million years ago.

2

1

Most **Ceratopsians** had horns, a beak, and a neck frill. Many were large and heavy, but there was a small **Ceratopsian** called **Brachyceratops** (BRACK-EE-SER-A-TOPS), which was smaller than a human.

The largest was **Triceratops horridus** (HOR-EE-DUS) **(1)**. Its name means "horrible three-horned face." It was nearly as long as a bus.

Pentaceratops (PEN-TA-SER-A-TOPS) **(2),** a cousin, has a name meaning "five-horned face," but it only had three horns. The scientists who first studied its skull mistook its pointed cheek bones for two extra horns.

It was 23 feet (7 m) long, quite a bit shorter than **Triceratops.** It had sharp, bony points all around the edge of its neck frill.

Styracosaurus (STY-RAK-OH-SAW-RUS) **(4)** was a little bigger than a family car. It had a long horn on its nose, but the horns on top of its head were quite small. It made up for this by having long, sharp spikes around the edge of its frill.

No one knows exactly how big **Torosaurus** (TOR-OH-SAW-RUS) **(3)** was. The only bones found so far are from its skull. But scientists think it must have had one of the most massive heads of any living creature. It was given a name meaning "bull lizard" because it had horns like a bull. It lived at about the same time as **Triceratops** and died out with all the other dinosaurs 65 million years ago.

3

4

GLOSSARY

carnivores — meat-eating animals.

frill — a fringe or ruffle around the neck of an animal.

graze — to feed on grass or other plants that grow in a field or pasture.

herd — a group of animals that travels and lives together.

knobby — covered with lumps, bumps, or bulges of some sort.

mate — to join together (animals) to produce young.

pads — soft, cushionlike parts on the undersides of some animals' feet or paws.

predators — animals that kill other animals for food.

reptiles — cold-blooded animals that have hornlike or scale-covered skin. Pterosaurs were flying reptiles.

INDEX